The True-Born En

A Satire

Daniel Defoe

Alpha Editions

This edition published in 2024

ISBN : 9789362099938

Design and Setting By
Alpha Editions
www.alphaedis.com
Email - info@alphaedis.com

As per information held with us this book is in Public Domain.
This book is a reproduction of an important historical work. Alpha Editions uses the best technology to reproduce historical work in the same manner it was first published to preserve its original nature. Any marks or number seen are left intentionally to preserve its true form.

Contents

AN EXPLANATORY PREFACE. .... - 1 -
PREFACE. .... - 5 -
THE INTRODUCTION. .... - 7 -
THE TRUE-BORN ENGLISHMAN. .... - 9 -
    PART I. .... - 9 -
    PART II. .... - 18 -
    BRITANNIA. .... - 29 -
    HIS FINE SPEECH, &c. .... - 34 -
    THE CONCLUSION. .... - 37 -
FOOTNOTES .... - 39 -

AN EXPLANATORY PREFACE.

It is not that I see any reason to alter my opinion in any thing I have writ, which occasions this epistle; but I find it necessary for the satisfaction of some persons of honour, as well as wit, to pass a short explication upon it; and tell the world what I mean, or rather, what I do not mean, in some things wherein I find I am liable to be misunderstood.

I confess myself something expris'd to hear that I am taxed with bewraying my own nest, and abusing our nation, by discovering the meanness of our original, in order to make the English contemptible abroad and at home; in which, I think, they are mistaken: for why should not our neighbours be as good as we to derive from? And I must add, that had we been an unmix'd nation, I am of opinion it had been to our disadvantage: for to go no farther, we have three nations about us as clear from mixtures of blood as any in the world, and I know not which of them I could wish ourselves to be like; I mean the Scots, the Welsh, and the Irish; and if I were to write a reverse to the Satire, I would examine all the nations of Europe, and prove, that those nations which are most mix'd, are the best, and have least of barbarism and brutality among them; and abundance of reasons might be given for it, too long to bring into a Preface.

But I give this hint, to let the world know, that I am far from thinking, 'tis a Satire upon the English nation, to tell them, they are derived from all the nations under heaven; that is, from several nations. Nor is it meant to undervalue the original of the English, for we see no reason to like them worse, being the relicts of Romans, Danes, Saxons and Normans, than we should have done if they had remain'd Britons, that is, than if they had been all Welshmen.

But the intent of the Satire is pointed at the vanity of those who talk of their antiquity, and value themselves upon their pedigree, their ancient families, and being true-born; whereas 'tis impossible we should be true-born: and if we could, should have lost by the bargain.

These sort of people, who call themselves true-born, and tell long stories of their families, and like a nobleman of Venice, think a foreigner ought not to walk on the same side of the street with them, are own'd to be meant in this Satire. What they would infer from their long original, I know not, nor is it easy to make out whether they are the better or the worse for their ancestors: our English nation may value themselves for their wit, wealth and courage, and I believe few nations will dispute it with them; but for long originals, and ancient true-born families of English, I would advise them to wave the discourse. A true Englishman is one that deserves a character, and I have nowhere lessened him, that I know of; but as for a true-born Englishman, I confess I do not understand him.

From hence I only infer, that an Englishman, of all men, ought not to despise foreigners as such, and I think the inference is just, since what they are to-day, we were yesterday, and to-morrow they will be like us. If foreigners misbehave in their several stations and employments, I have nothing to do with that; the laws are open to punish them equally with natives, and let them have no favour.

But when I see the town full of lampoons and invectives against Dutchmen, only because they are foreigners, and the king reproached and insulted by insolent pedants, and ballad-making poets, for employing foreigners, and for being a foreigner himself, I confess myself moved by it to remind our nation of their own original, thereby to let them see what a banter is put upon ourselves in it; since speaking of Englishmen *ab origine*, we are really all foreigners ourselves.

I could go on to prove it is also impolitic in us to discourage foreigners; since it is easy to make it appear that the multitudes of foreign nations who have taken sanctuary here, have been the greatest additions to the wealth and strength of the nation; the essential whereof is the number of its inhabitants; nor would this nation ever have arrived to the degree of wealth and glory it now boasts of, if the addition of foreign nations, both as to manufactures and arms, had not been helpful to it. This is so plain, that he who is ignorant of it, is too dull to be talked with.

The Satire therefore I must allow to be just, till I am otherwise convinced; because nothing can be more ridiculous than to hear our people boast of that antiquity, which if it had been true, would have left us in so much worse a condition than we are in now: whereas we ought rather to boast among our neighbours, that we are part of themselves, of the same original as they, but bettered by our climate, and like our language and manufactures, derived from them, and improved by us to a perfection greater than they can pretend to.

This we might have valued ourselves upon without vanity; but to disown our descent from them, talk big of our ancient families, and long originals, and stand at a distance from foreigners, like the enthusiast in religion, with a Stand off, I am more holy than thou: this is a thing so ridiculous, in a nation derived from foreigners, as we are, that I could not but attack them as I have done.

And whereas I am threatened to be called to a public account for this freedom; and the publisher of this has been newspapered into gaol already for it; tho' I see nothing in it for which the government can be displeased; yet if at the same time those people who with an unlimited arrogance in print, every day affront the king, prescribe the parliament, and lampoon the government, may be either punished or restrained, I am content to stand and fall by the public justice of my native country, which I am not sensible I have anywhere injured.

Nor would I be misunderstood concerning the clergy; with whom, if I have taken any license more than becomes a Satire, I question not but those gentlemen, who are men of letters, are also men of so much candor, as to allow me a loose at the crimes of the guilty, without thinking the whole profession lashed who are innocent. I profess to have very mean thoughts of those gentlemen who have deserted their own principles, and exposed even their morals as well as loyalty; but not at all to think it affects any but such as are concerned in the fact.

Nor would I be misrepresented as to the ingratitude of the English to the king and his friends; as if I meant the English as a nation, are so. The contrary is so apparent, that I would hope it should not be suggested of me: and, therefore when I have brought in Britannia speaking of the king, I suppose her to be the representative or mouth of the nation, as a body. But if I say we are full of such who daily affront the king, and abuse his friends; who print scurrilous pamphlets, virulent lampoons, and reproachful public banters, against both the king's person and his government; I say nothing but what is too true; and that the Satire is directed at such, I freely own; and cannot say, but I should think it very hard to be censured for this Satire, while such remain unquestioned and tacitly approved. That I can mean none but such, is plain from these few lines, page 453.

> Ye heavens regard! Almighty Jove, look down,
> And view thy injured monarch on the throne.
> On their ungrateful heads due vengeance take,
> Who sought his aid, and then his part forsake.

If I have fallen rudely upon our vices, I hope none but the vicious will be angry. As for writing for interest, I disown it; I have neither place, nor pension, nor prospect; nor seek none, nor will have none: if matter of fact justifies the truth of the crimes, the Satire is just. As to the poetic liberties, I hope the crime is pardonable; I am content to be stoned, provided none will attack me but the innocent.

If my countrymen would take the hint, and grow better natured from my ill-natured poem as some call it; I would say this of it, that though it is far from the best Satire that ever was wrote, it would do the most good that ever Satire did.

And yet I am ready to ask pardon of some gentlemen too; who though they are Englishmen, have good nature enough to see themselves reproved, and can hear it. These are gentlemen in a true sense, that can bare to be told of their *faux pas*, and not abuse the reprover. To such I must say, this is no Satire; they are exceptions to the general rule; and I value my performance from their generous approbation, more than I can from any opinion I have of its worth.

The hasty errors of my verse I made my excuse for before; and since the time I have been upon it has been but little, and my leisure less, I have all along strove rather to make the thoughts explicit, than the poem correct. However, I have mended some faults in this edition, and the rest must be placed to my account.

As to answers, banters, true English Billingsgate, I expect them till nobody will buy, and then the shop will be shut. Had I wrote it for the gain of the press, I should have been concerned at its being printed again, and again, by pirates, as they call them, and paragraph-men; but would they but do it justice, and print it true, according to the copy, they are welcome to sell it for a penny, if they please.

The pence, indeed, is the end of their works. I will engage if nobody will buy, nobody will write: and not a patriot poet of them all, now will in defence of his native country, which I have abused, they say, print an answer to it, and give it about for God's sake.

PREFACE.

THE end of satire is reformation: and the author, though he doubt the work of conversion is at a general stop, has put his hand in the plough. I expect a storm of ill language from the fury of the town. And especially from those whose English talent it is to rail: and, without being taken for a conjuror, I may venture to foretel, that I shall be cavilled at about my mean style, rough verse, and incorrect language, things I indeed might have taken more care in. But the book is printed; and though I see some faults, it is too late to mend them. And this is all I think needful to say to them.

Possibly somebody may take me for a Dutchman; in which they are mistaken: but I am one that would be glad to see Englishmen behave themselves better to strangers, and to governors also, that one might not be reproached in foreign countries for belonging to a nation that wants manners.

I assure you, gentlemen, strangers use us better abroad; and we can give no reason but our ill-nature for the contrary here.

Methinks an Englishman who is so proud of being called a good fellow, should be civil. And it cannot be denied, but we are, in many cases, and particularly to strangers, the most churlish people alive.

As to vices, who can dispute our intemperance, while an honest drunken fellow is a character in a man's praise? All our reformations are banters, and will be so till our magistrates and gentry reform themselves, by way of example; then, and not till then, they may be expected to punish others without blushing.

As to our ingratitude, I desire to be understood of that particular people, who pretending to be Protestants, have all along endeavoured to reduce the liberties and religion of this nation into the hands of King James and his Popish powers: together with such who enjoy the peace and protection of the present government, and yet abuse and affront the king who procured it, and openly profess their uneasiness under him: these, by whatsoever names or titles they are dignified or distinguished, are the people aimed at; nor do I disown, but that it is so much the temper of an Englishman to abuse his benefactor, that I could be glad to see it rectified.

They who think I have been guilty of any error, in exposing the crimes of my own countrymen to themselves, may, among many honest instances of the like nature, find the same thing in Mr. Cowley, in his imitation of the second Olympic Ode of Pindar; his words are these:—

But in this thankless world, the givers
Are envied even by the receivers.
'Tis now the cheap and frugal fashion,
Rather to hide than pay an obligation.
Nay, 'tis much worse than so;
It now an artifice doth grow,
Wrongs and outrages they do,
Lest men should think we owe.

THE INTRODUCTION.

SPEAK, Satire, for there's none can tell like thee,
Whether 'tis folly, pride, or knavery,
That makes this discontented land appear
Less happy now in times of peace, than war:
Why civil feuds disturb the nation more,
Than all our bloody wars have done before.

FOOLS out of favour grudge at knaves in place,
And men are always honest in disgrace:
The court preferments make men knaves in course:
But they which wou'd be in them wou'd be worse.
'Tis not at foreigners that we repine,
Wou'd foreigners their perquisites resign:
The grand contention's plainly to be seen,
To get some men put out, and some put in.
For this our Senators make long harangues.
And florid Ministers whet their polish'd tongues.
Statesmen are always sick of one disease;
And a good pension gives them present ease.
That's the specific makes them all content
With any King and any government.
Good patriots at court abuses rail,
And all the nation's grievances bewail:
But when the sov'reign balsam's once apply'd,
The zealot never fails to change his side;
And when he must the golden key resign,
The railing spirit comes about again.

WHO shall this bubbl'd nation disabuse,
While they their own felicities refuse?
Who at the wars have made such mighty pother,
And now are falling out with one another:
With needless fears the jealous nations fill,
And always have been sav'd against their will:
Who fifty millions sterling have disburs'd
To be with peace, and too much plenty, curs'd;
Who their old monarch eagerly undo,
And yet uneasily obey the new.
Search, Satire, search; a deep incision make:

The poison's strong, the antidote's too weak.
'Tis pointed truth must manage this dispute,
And down-right English, Englishmen confute.

WHET thy just anger at the nation's pride;
And with keen phrase repel the vicious tide,
To Englishmen their own beginnings show,
And ask them, why they slight their neighbours so:
Go back to elder times, and ages past,
And nations into long oblivion cast;
To elder Britain's youthful days retire,
And there for true-born Englishmen inquire,
Britannia freely will disown the name,
And hardly knows herself from whence they came;
Wonders that they of all men should pretend
To birth, and blood, and for a name contend.
Go back to causes where our follies dwell,
And fetch the dark original from hell:
Speak, Satire, for there's none like thee can tell.

THE TRUE-BORN ENGLISHMAN.

PART I.

WHEREVER God erects a house of prayer,
The Devil always builds a chapel there:
And 'twill be found upon examination,
The latter has the largest congregation:
For ever since he first debauch'd the mind,
He made a perfect conquest of mankind.
With uniformity of service, he
Reigns with general aristocracy.
No non-conforming sects disturb his reign,
For of his yoke, there's very few complain.
He knows the genius and the inclination,
And matches proper sins for ev'ry nation.
He needs no standing army government;
He always rules us by our own consent:
His laws are easy, and his gentle sway
Makes it exceeding pleasant to obey.
The list of his vicegerents and commanders,
Out-does your Cæsars, or your Alexanders.
They never fail of his infernal aid,
And he's as certain ne'er to be betray'd.
Thro' all the world they spread his vast command,
And death's eternal empire is maintain'd.
They rule so politicly and so well,
As if they were Lords Justices of hell;
Duly divided to debauch mankind,
And plant infernal dictates in his mind.

PRIDE, the first peer, and president of hell,
To his share, Spain, the largest province fell.
The subtle Prince thought fittest to bestow
On these the golden mines of Mexico,
With all the silver mountains of Peru;
Wealth which in wise hands would the world undo;
Because he knew their genius was such,
Too lazy and too haughty to be rich:
So proud a people, so above their fate,
That, if reduced to beg, they'll beg in state:
Lavish of money, to be counted brave,

And proudly starve, because they scorn to save;
Never was nation in the world before,
So very rich, and yet so very poor.

LUST chose the torrid zone of Italy,
Where blood ferments in rapes and sodomy:
Where swelling veins o'erflow with living streams,
With heat impregnate from Vesuvian flames;
Whose flowing sulphur forms infernal lakes,
And human body of the soil partakes.
There nature ever burns with hot desires,
Fann'd with luxuriant air from subterranean fires:
Here undisturbed, in floods of scalding lust,
Th' infernal king reigns with infernal gust.

DRUNKENNESS, the darling favourite of hell,
Chose Germany to rule; and rules so well,
No subjects more obsequiously obey,
None please so well, or are so pleased as they;
The cunning artist manages so well,
He lets them bow to heav'n, and drink to hell.
If but to wine and him they homage pay,
He cares not to what deity they pray;
What god they worship most, or in what way.
Whether by Luther, Calvin, or by Rome,
They sail for heaven, by wine he steers them home.

UNGOVERN'D PASSION settled first in France,
Where mankind lives in haste, and thrives by chance;
A dancing nation, fickle and untrue,
Have oft undone themselves, and others too;
Prompt the infernal dictates to obey,
And in hell's favour none more great than they.

THE pagan world he blindly leads away,
And personally rules with arbitrary sway:
The mask thrown off, plain devil, his title stands;
And what elsewhere he tempts, he there commands;
There, with full gust, th' ambition of his mind,
Governs, as he of old in heaven design'd:
Worshipp'd as God, his Paynim altars smoke,
Imbrued with blood of those that him invoke.

THE rest by deputies he rules so well,
And plants the distant colonies of hell;
By them his secret power he firm maintains,
And binds the world in his infernal chains.

BY zeal the Irish, and the Russ by folly,
Fury the Dane, the Swede by melancholy;
By stupid ignorance, the Muscovite;
The Chinese, by a child of hell, call'd wit;
Wealth makes the Persian too effeminate;
And poverty the Tartar desperate:
The Turks and Moors, by Mah'met he subdues;
And God has given him leave to rule the Jews:
Rage rules the Portuguese, and fraud the Scotch;
Revenge the Pole, and avarice the Dutch.

SATIRE, be kind, and draw a silent veil,
Thy native England's vices to conceal:
Or, if that task's impossible to do,
At least be just, and show her virtues too;
Too great the first, alas! the last too few.

ENGLAND, unknown, as yet unpeopled lay,—
Happy, had she remain'd so to this day,
And still to ev'ry nation been a prey.
Her open harbours, and her fertile plains,
The merchant's glory these, and those the swain's,
To ev'ry barbarous nation have betray'd her;
Who conquer her as oft as they invade her,
So beauty, guarded out by Innocence,
That ruins her which should be her defence.

INGRATITUDE, a devil of black renown,
Possess'd her very early for his own:
An ugly, surly, sullen, selfish spirit,
Who Satan's worst perfections does inherit;
Second to him in malice and in force,
All devil without, and all within him worse.

HE made her first-born race to be so rude,
And suffer'd her to be so oft subdued;
By sev'ral crowds of wandering thieves o'er-run,
Often unpeopled, and as oft undone;

While ev'ry nation that her powers reduced,
Their languages and manners introduced;
From whose mix'd relics our compounded breed,
By spurious generation does succeed;
Making a race uncertain and uneven,
Derived from all the nations under heaven.

THE Romans first with Julius Cæsar came,
Including all the nations of that name,
Gauls, Greek, and Lombards; and, by computation,
Auxiliaries or slaves of ev'ry nation.
With Hengist, Saxons; Danes with Sweno came,
In search of plunder, not in search of fame.
Scots, Picts, and Irish from th' Hibernian shore;
And conq'ring William brought the Normans o'er.

ALL these their barb'rous offspring left behind,
The dregs of armies, they of all mankind;
Blended with Britons, who before were here,
Of whom the Welch ha' blest the character.

FROM this amphibious, ill-born mob began,
That vain ill-natured thing, an Englishman.
The customs, sirnames, languages, and manners,
Of all these nations, are their own explainers;
Whose relics are so lasting and so strong,
They've left a Shiboleth upon our tongue;
By which, with easy search, you may distinguish
Your Roman, Saxon, Danish, Norman, English.

THE great invading Norman let us know
What conquerors in after-times might do.
To every musqueteer he brought to town,
He gave the lands which never were his own;
When first the English crown he did obtain,
He did not send his Dutchmen home again.
No re-assumptions in his reign were known,
Davenant might there ha' let his book alone.
No parliament his army could disband;
He raised no money, for he paid in land.
He gave his legions their eternal station,
And made them all freeholders of the nation.
He canton'd out the country to his men,

And every soldier was a denizen.
The rascals thus enrich'd, he called them lords,
To please their upstart pride with new-made words,
And doomsday book his tyranny records.

AND here begins the ancient pedigree
That so exalts our poor nobility.
'Tis that from some French trooper they derive,
Who with the Norman bastard did arrive:
The trophies of the families appear;
Some show the sword, the bow, and some the spear,
Which their great ancestor, forsooth, did wear.
These in the herald's register remain,
Their noble mean extraction to explain,
Yet who the hero was no man can tell,
Whether a drummer or a colonel:
The silent record blushes to reveal
Their undescended dark original.

BUT grant the best. How came the change to pass;
A true-born Englishman of Norman race?
A Turkish horse can show more history,
To prove his well-descended family.
Conquest, as by the moderns 'tis express'd,
May give a title to the lands possess'd;
But that the longest sword should be so civil,
To make a Frenchman English, that's the devil.

THESE are the heroes that despise the Dutch,
And rail at new-come foreigners so much;
Forgetting that themselves are all derived
From the most scoundrel race that ever lived;
A horrid crowd of rambling thieves and drones
Who ransack'd kingdoms, and dispeopled towns;
The Pict and painted Briton, treach'rous Scot,
By hunger, theft, and rapine, hither brought;
Norwegian pirates, buccaneering Danes,
Whose red-hair'd offspring everywhere remains;
Who, join'd with Norman French, compound the breed
From whence your true-born Englishmen proceed.

AND lest, by length of time, it be pretended,
The climate may this modern breed have mended;

Wise Providence, to keep us where we are,
Mixes us daily with exceeding care;
We have been Europe's sink, the jakes, where she
Voids all her offal out-cast progeny;
From our fifth Henry's time the strolling bands,
Of banish'd fugitives from neighb'ring lands,
Have here a certain sanctuary found:
The eternal refuge of the vagabond,
Where in but half a common age of time,
Borrowing new blood and manners from the clime,
Proudly they learn all mankind to contemn,
And all their race are true-born Englishmen.

DUTCH Walloons, Flemmings, Irishmen, and Scots,
Vaudois, and Valtolins, and Hugonots,
In good Queen Bess's charitable reign,
Supplied us with three hundred thousand men:
Religion—God, we thank thee!—sent them hither,
Priests, Protestants, the devil, and all together;
Of all professions, and of ev'ry trade,
All that were persecuted or afraid:
Whether for debt, or other crimes, they fled,
David at Hackelah was still their head.

THE offspring of this miscellaneous crowd,
Had not their new plantations long enjoy'd,
But they grew Englishmen, and raised their votes,
At foreign shoals of interloping Scots;
The royal branch from Pict-land did succeed,
With troops of Scots and scabs from north of Tweed;
The seven first years of his pacific reign,
Made him and half his nation Englishmen.
Scots from the northern frozen banks of Tay,
With packs and plods came whigging all away,
Thick as the locusts which in Egypt swarm'd,
With pride and hungry hopes completely arm'd;
With native truth, diseases, and no money,
Plunder'd our Canaan of the milk and honey;
Here they grew quickly lords and gentlemen,
And all their race are true-born Englishmen.

THE civil wars, the common purgative,
Which always use to make the nation thrive,

Made way for all that strolling congregation,
Which throng'd in pious Charles's restoration.
The royal refugee our breed restores,
With foreign courtiers, and with foreign whores:
And carefully re-peopled us again,
Throughout his lazy, long, lascivious reign,
With such a blest and true-born English fry,
As much illustrates our nobility.
A gratitude which will so black appear,
As future ages must abhor to bear:
When they look back on all that crimson flood,
Which stream'd in Lindsey's, and Caernarvon's blood;
Bold Strafford, Cambridge, Capel, Lucas, Lisle,
Who crown'd in death his father's fun'ral pile.
The loss of whom, in order to supply
With true-born English nobility,
Six bastard dukes survive his luscious reign,
The labours of Italian Castlemain,
French Portsmouth, Tabby Scott, and Cambrian;
Besides the num'rous bright and virgin throng,
Whose female glories shade them from my song.
This offspring if our age they multiply,
May half the house with English peers supply:
There with true English pride they may contemn
Schomberg and Portland, new-made noblemen.

FRENCH cooks, Scotch pedlars, and Italian whores,
Were all made lords or lords' progenitors.
Beggars and bastards by this new creation
Much multiplied the peerage of the nation;
Who will be all, ere one short age runs o'er,
As true-born lords as those we had before.

THEN to recruit the commons he prepares,
And heal the latent breaches of the wars;
The pious purpose better to advance,
He invites the banish'd Protestants of France;
Hither for God's sake, and their own, they fled
Some for religion came, and some for bread:
Two hundred thousand pair of wooden shoes,
Who, God be thank'd, had nothing left to lose;
To heaven's great praise did for religion fly,
To make us starve our poor in charity.

In ev'ry port they plant their fruitful train,
To get a race of true-born Englishmen;
Whose children will, when riper years they see,
Be as ill-natured, and as proud as we;
Call themselves English, foreigners despise,
Be surly like us all, and just as wise.

THUS from a mixture of all kinds began,
That heterogeneous thing, an Englishman:
In eager rapes, and furious lust begot,
Betwixt a painted Briton and a Scot:
Whose gend'ring offspring quickly learn'd to bow,
And yoke their heifers to the Roman plough;
From whence a mongrel half-bred race there came,
With neither name nor nation, speech or fame,
In whose hot veins new mixtures quickly ran,
Infused betwixt a Saxon and a Dane;
While their rank daughters, to their parents just,
Received all nations with promiscuous lust.
This nauseous brood directly did contain
The well-extracted blood of Englishmen.

WHICH medley, canton'd in a heptarchy,
A rhapsody of nations to supply,
Among themselves maintain'd eternal wars,
And still the ladies loved the conquerors.

THE Western Angles all the rest subdued,
A bloody nation, barbarous and rude;
Who by the tenure of the sword possess'd
One part of Britain, and subdued the rest:
And as great things denominate the small,
The conquering part gave title to the whole;
The Scot, Pict, Briton, Roman, Dane, submit,
And with the English Saxon all unite:
And these the mixture have so close pursued,
The very name and memory's subdued;
No Roman now, no Briton does remain;
Wales strove to separate, but strove in vain:
The silent nations undistinguish'd fall,
And Englishman's the common name for all.
Fate jumbled them together, God knows how;
Whate'er they were, they're true-born English now.

THE wonder which remains is at our pride,
To value that which all wise men deride;
For Englishmen to boast of generation
Cancels their knowledge, and lampoons the nation,
A true-born Englishman's a contradiction,
In speech an irony, in fact a fiction:
A banter made to be a test of fools,
Which those that use it justly ridicules;
A metaphor intended to express,
A man a-kin to all the universe.

FOR as the Scots, as learned men have said,
Throughout the world their wand'ring seed have spread,
So open-handed England, 'tis believed,
Has all the gleanings of the world received.

SOME think of England, 'twas our Saviour meant,
The Gospel should to all the world be sent:
Since when the blessed sound did hither reach,
They to all nations might be said to preach.

'TIS well that virtue gives nobility,
Else God knows where had we our gentry,
Since scarce one family is left alive,
Which does not from some foreigner derive.
Of sixty thousand English gentlemen,
Whose names and arms in registers remain,
We challenge all our heralds to declare
Ten families which English Saxons are.

FRANCE justly boasts the ancient noble line
Of Bourbon, Montmorency, and Lorraine.
The Germans too, their house of Austria show,
And Holland, their invincible Nassau.
Lines which in heraldry were ancient grown,
Before the name of Englishman was known.
Even Scotland, too, her elder glory shows,
Her Gordons, Hamiltons, and her Monro's;
Douglas', Mackays, and Grahams, names well known,
Long before ancient England knew her own.

BUT England, modern to the last degree,
Borrows or makes her own nobility,

And yet she boldly boasts of pedigree;
Repines that foreigners are put upon her,
And talks of her antiquity and honour:
Her Sackvills, Savils, Cecils, Delamers,
Mohuns, Montagues, Duras, and Veeres,
Not one have English names, yet all are English peers.
Your Houblons, Papillons, and Lethuliers,
Pass now for true-born English knights and squires,
And make good senate-members, or lord-mayors.
Wealth, howsoever got, in England makes
Lords of mechanics, gentlemen of rakes.
Antiquity and birth are needless here;
'Tis impudence and money makes a peer.

INNUMERABLE city knights we know,
From Blue-coat Hospitals, and Bridewell flow.
Draymen and porters fill the city chair,
And foot-boys magisterial purple wear.
Fate has but very small distinction set
Betwixt the counter and the coronet.
Tarpaulin lords, pages of high renown,
Rise up by poor men's valour, not their own;
Great families of yesterday we show,
And lords, whose parents were the Lord knows who.

PART II.

THE breed's described: now, Satire, if you can,
Their temper show, for manners make the man.
Fierce as the Briton, as the Roman brave,
And less inclined to conquer than to save;
Eager to fight, and lavish of their blood,
And equally of fear and forecast void.
The Pict has made them sour, the Dane morose,
False from the Scot, and from the Norman worse.
What honesty they have, the Saxon gave them,
And that, now they grow old, begins to leave them.
The climate makes them terrible and bold:
And English beef their courage does uphold:
No danger can their daring spirit dull,
Always provided when their belly's full.

IN close intrigues, their faculty's but weak;

For, gen'rally, whate'er they know they speak.
And often their own councils undermine
By their infirmity, and not design.
From whence, the learned say, it does proceed,
That English treason never can succeed:
For they're so open-hearted, you may know
Their own most secret thoughts, and others too.

THE lab'ring poor, in spite of double pay,
Are saucy, mutinous, and beggarly;
So lavish of their money and their time,
That want of forecast is the nation's crime.
Good drunken company is their delight;
And what they get by day they spend by night.
Dull thinking seldom does their heads engage,
But drink their youth away, and hurry on old age.
Empty of all good husbandry and sense;
And void of manners most when void of pence.
Their strong aversion to behaviour's such,
They always talk too little or too much.
So dull, they never take the pains to think;
And seldom are good natured but in drink.

IN English ale their dear enjoyment lies,
For which they starve themselves and families.
An Englishman will fairly drink as much,
As will maintain two families of Dutch:
Subjecting all their labours to the pots;
The greatest artists are the greatest sots.
The country poor do by example live;
The gentry lead them, and the clergy drive;
What may we not from such examples hope?
The landlord is their god, the priest their pope;
A drunken clergy, and a swearing bench,
Has given the reformation such a drench,
As wise men think, there is some cause to doubt,
Will purge good manners and religion out.

NOR do the poor alone their liquor prize,
The sages join in this great sacrifice;
The learned men who study Aristotle,
Correct him with an explanation bottle:
Praise Epicurus rather than Lysander,

And Aristippus more than Alexander;
The doctors too their Galen here resign,
And generally prescribe specific wine;
The graduate's study's grown an easy task,
While for the urinal they toss the flask;
The surgeon's art grows plainer every hour,
And wine's the balm which into wounds they pour.

POETS long since Parnassus have forsaken,
And say the ancient bards were all mistaken.
Apollo's lately abdicate and fled,
And good king Bacchus reigneth in his stead:
He does the chaos of the head refine,
And atom thoughts jump into words by wine:
The inspiration's of a finer nature,
As wine must needs excel Parnassus water.

STATESMEN their weighty politics refine,
And soldiers raise their courages by wine.
Cecilia gives her choristers their choice,
And lets them all drink wine to clear the voice.

SOME think the clergy first found out the way,
And wine's the only spirit by which they pray.
But others, less profane than so, agree,
It clears the lungs, and helps the memory:
And, therefore, all of them divinely think,
Instead of study, 'tis as well to drink.

AND here I would be very glad to know,
Whether our Asgilites may drink or no;
The enlightening fumes of wine would certainly
Assist them much when they begin to fly;
Or if a fiery chariot should appear,
Inflamed by wine, they'd have the less to fear.

EVEN the gods themselves, as mortals say,
Were they on earth, would be as drunk as they:
Nectar would be no more celestial drink,
They'd all take wine, to teach them how to think.
But English drunkards, gods and men outdo,
Drink their estates away, and senses too.
Colon's in debt, and if his friend should fail

To help him out, must die at last in jail:
His wealthy uncle sent a hundred nobles,
To pay his trifles off, and rid him of his troubles:
But Colon, like a true-born Englishman,
Drunk all the money out in bright champaign,
And Colon does in custody remain.
Drunk'ness has been the darling of the realm,
E'er since a drunken pilot had the helm.

IN their religion, they're so uneven,
That each man goes his own byway to heaven.
Tenacious of mistakes to that degree,
That ev'ry man pursues it sep'rately,
And fancies none can find the way but he:
So shy of one another they are grown,
As if they strove to get to heaven alone.
Rigid and zealous, positive and grave,
And ev'ry grace, but charity, they have;
This makes them so ill-natured and uncivil,
That all men think an Englishman the devil.

SURLY to strangers, froward to their friend,
Submit to love with a reluctant mind,
Resolved to be ungrateful and unkind.
If, by necessity, reduced to ask,
The giver has the difficultest task:
For what's bestow'd they awkwardly receive,
And always take less freely than they give;
The obligation is their highest grief,
They never love where they accept relief;
So sullen in their sorrows, that 'tis known
They'll rather die than their afflictions own;
And if relieved, it is too often true,
That they'll abuse their benefactors too;
For in distress their haughty stomach's such,
They hate to see themselves obliged too much;
Seldom contented, often in the wrong,
Hard to be pleased at all, and never long.

IF your mistakes there ill opinion gain,
No merit can their favour re-obtain:
And if they're not vindictive in their fury,
'Tis their inconstant temper does secure ye:

Their brain's so cool, their passion seldom burns;
For all's condensed before the flame returns:
The fermentation's of so weak a matter,
The humid damps the flame, and runs it all to water;
So though the inclination may be strong,
They're pleased by fits, and never angry long:

THEN, if good-nature show some slender proof,
They never think they have reward enough;
But, like our modern Quakers of the town,
Expect your manners, and return you none.

FRIENDSHIP, th' abstracted union of the mind,
Which all men seek, but very few can find;
Of all the nations in the universe,
None can talk on't more, or understand it less;
For if it does their property annoy,
Their property their friendship will destroy.
As you discourse them, you shall hear them tell
All things in which they think they do excel:
No panegyric needs their praise record,
An Englishman ne'er wants his own good word.
His first discourses gen'rally appear,
Prologued with his own wond'rous character:
When, to illustrate his own good name,
He never fails his neighbour to defame.
And yet he really designs no wrong,
His malice goes no further than his tongue.
But, pleased to tattle, he delights to rail,
To satisfy the letch'ry of a tale.
His own dear praises close the ample speech,
Tells you how wise he is, that is, how rich:
For wealth is wisdom; he that's rich is wise;
And all men learned poverty despise:
His generosity comes next, and then
Concludes, that he's a true-born Englishman;
And they, 'tis known, are generous and free,
Forgetting, and forgiving injury:
Which may be true, thus rightly understood,
Forgiving ill turns, and forgetting good.

CHEERFUL in labour when they've undertook it,
But out of humour, when they're out of pocket.

But if their belly and their pocket's full,
They may be phlegmatic, but never dull:
And if a bottle does their brains refine,
It makes their wit as sparkling as their wine.

AS for the general vices which we find,
They're guilty of in common with mankind,
Satire forbear, and silently endure,
We must conceal the crimes we cannot cure;
Nor shall my verse the brighter sex defame,
For English beauty will preserve her name;
Beyond dispute agreeable and fair,
And modester than other nations are;
For where the vice prevails, the great temptation
Is want of money more than inclination;
In general this only is allow'd,
They're something noisy, and a little proud.

AN Englishman is gentlest in command,
Obedience is a stranger in the land:
Hardly subjected to the magistrate;
For Englishmen do all subjection hate.
Humblest when rich, but peevish when they're poor,
And think whate'er they have, they merit more.

THE meanest English plowman studies law,
And keeps thereby the magistrates in awe,
Will boldly tell them what they ought to do,
And sometimes punish their omissions too.

THEIR liberty and property's so dear,
They scorn their laws or governors to fear;
So bugbear'd with the name of slavery,
They can't submit to their own liberty.
Restraint from ill is freedom to the wise!
But Englishmen do all restraint despise.
Slaves to the liquor, drudges to the pots;
The mob are statesmen, and their statesmen sots.

THEIR governors, they count such dang'rous things,
That 'tis their custom to affront their kings:
So jealous of the power their kings possess'd,
They suffer neither power nor kings to rest.

The bad with force they eagerly subdue;
The good with constant clamours they pursue,
And did King Jesus reign, they'd murmur too.
A discontented nation, and by far
Harder to rule in times of peace than war:
Easily set together by the ears,
And full of causeless jealousies and fears:
Apt to revolt, and willing to rebel,
And never are contented when they're well.
No government could ever please them long,
Could tie their hands, or rectify their tongue.
In this, to ancient Israel well compared,
Eternal murmurs are among them heard.

IT was but lately, that they were oppress'd,
Their rights invaded, and their laws suppress'd:
When nicely tender of their liberty,
Lord! what a noise they made of slavery.
In daily tumults show'd their discontent,
Lampoon'd their king, and mock'd his government.
And if in arms they did not first appear,
'Twas want of force, and not for want of fear.
In humbler tone than English used to do,
At foreign hands for foreign aid they sue.

WILLIAM, the great successor of Nassau,
Their prayers heard, and their oppressions saw;
He saw and saved them: God and him they praised
To this their thanks, to that their trophies raised.
But glutted with their own felicities,
They soon their new deliverer despise;
Say all their prayers back, their joy disown,
Unsing their thanks, and pull their trophies down;
Their harps of praise are on the willows hung;
For Englishmen are ne'er contented long.

THE reverend clergy too, and who'd ha' thought
That they who had such non-resistance taught,
Should e'er to arms against their prince be brought
Who up to heav'n did regal power advance;
Subjecting English laws to modes of France
Twisting religion so with loyalty,
As one could never live, and t'other die;

And yet no sooner did their prince design
Their glebes and perquisites to undermine,
But all their passive doctrines laid aside,
The clergy their own principles denied;
Unpreach'd their non-resisting cant, and pray'd
To heav'n for help, and to the Dutch for aid;
The church chimed all her doctrines back again,
And pulpit-champions did the cause maintain;
Flew in the face of all their former zeal,
And non-resistance did at once repeal.

THE Rabbi's say it would be too prolix,
To tie religion up to politics,
The churches' safety is *suprema lex*:
And so by a new figure of their own,
Their former doctrines all at once disown;
As laws *post facto* in the parliament,
In urgent cases have attained assent;
But are as dangerous precedents laid by,
Made lawful only by necessity.

THE rev'rend fathers then in arms appear,
And men of God became the men of war:
The nation, fired by them, to arms apply,
Assault their antichristian monarchy;
To their due channel all our laws restore,
And made things what they should have been before.
But when they came to fill the vacant throne,
And the pale priests look'd back on what they'd done,
How England liberty began to thrive,
And Church of England loyalty outlive;
How all their persecuting days were done,
And their deliv'rer placed upon the throne:
The priests, as priests are wont to do, turn'd tail,
They're Englishmen, and nature will prevail;
Now they deplore their ruins they have made,
And murmur for the master they betray'd;
Excuse those crimes they could not make him mend,
And suffer for the cause they can't defend;
Pretend they'd not have carried things so high,
And proto-martyrs make for popery.

HAD the prince done as they design'd the thing,

High set the clergy up to rule the king:
Taken a donative for coming hither,
And so have left their king and them together;
We had, say they, been now a happy nation;
No doubt we had seen a blessed reformation:
For wise men say 'tis as dangerous a thing,
A ruling priesthood, as a priest-rid king;
And of all plagues with which mankind are curst,
Ecclesiastic tyranny's the worst.

IF all our former grievances were feign'd,
King James has been abused, and we trepann'd;
Bugbear'd with popery and power despotic,
Tyrannic government, and leagues exotic;
The revolution's a fanatic plot,
William's a tyrant, King James was not;
A factious army and a poison'd nation,
Unjustly forced King James's abdication.

BUT if he did the subjects' rights invade,
Then he was punish'd only, not betrayed;
And punishing of kings is no such crime,
But Englishmen have done it many a time.

WHEN kings the sword of justice first lay down,
They are no kings, though they possess the crown.
Titles are shadows, crowns are empty things,
The good of subjects is the end of kings;
To guide in war, and to protect in peace,
Where tyrants once commence the kings do cease;
For arbitrary power's so strange a thing,
It makes the tyrant and unmakes the king:
If kings by foreign priests and armies reign,
And lawless power against their oaths maintain,
Then subjects must have reason to complain:
If oaths must bind us when our kings do ill,
To call in foreign aid is to rebel:
By force to circumscribe our lawful prince,
Is wilful treason in the largest sense:
And they who once rebel, must certainly
Their God, and king, and former oaths defy;
If ye allow no mal-administration
Could cancel the allegiance of the nation,

Let all our learned sons of Levi try,
This ecclesiastic riddle to untie;
How they could make a step to call the prince,
And yet pretend the oath and innocence.

BY th' first address they made beyond the seas,
They're perjur'd in the most intense degrees;
And without scruple for the time to come,
May swear to all the kings in Christendom:
Nay, truly did our kings consider all,
They'd never let the clergy swear at all,
Their politic allegiance they'd refuse,
For whores and priests do never want excuse.

BUT if the mutual contract was dissolved,
The doubt's explain'd, the difficulty solved;
That kings, when they descend to tyranny,
Dissolve the bond, and leave the subject free;
The government's ungirt when justice dies,
And constitutions are nonentities.
The nation's all a mob, there's no such thing,
As lords, or commons, parliament, or king;
A great promiscuous crowd the Hydra lies,
Till laws revive and mutual contract ties;
A chaos free to choose for their own share,
What case of government they please to wear;
If to a king they do the reins commit,
All men are bound in conscience to submit;
But then the king must by his oath assent,
To *Postulata's* of the government;
Which if he breaks he cuts off the entail,
And power retreats to its original.

THIS doctrine has the sanction of assent
From nature's universal Parliament:
The voice of nations, and the course of things,
Allow that laws superior are to kings;
None but delinquents would have justice cease,
Knaves rail at laws, as soldiers rail at peace:
For justice is the end of government,
As reason is the test of argument:
No man was ever yet so void of sense,
As to debate the right of self-defence;

A principle so grafted in the mind,
With nature born, and does like nature bind;
Twisted with reason, and with nature too,
As neither one nor t'other can undo.

NOR can this right be less when national,
Reason which governs one should govern all;
Whate'er the dialect of courts may tell,
He that his right demands can ne'er rebel;
Which right, if 'tis by governors denied,
May be procured by force or foreign aid;
For tyranny's a nation's term of grief,
As folks cry fire to hasten in relief;
And when the hated word is heard about,
All men should come to help the people out.

THUS England groan'd, Britannia's voice was heard,
And great Nassau to rescue her appear'd:
Call'd by the universal voice of fate,
God and the people's legal magistrate:
Ye heavens regard! Almighty Jove look down,
And view thy injured monarch on the throne;
On their ungrateful heads due vengeance take
Who sought his aid, and then his part forsake:
Witness, ye powers! it was our call alone,
Which now our pride makes us ashamed to own;
Britannia's troubles fetch'd him from afar,
To court the dreadful casualties of war;
But where requital never can be made,
Acknowledgment's a tribute seldom paid.

HE dwelt in bright Maria's circling arms,
Defended by the magic of her charms,
From foreign fears and from domestic harms;
Ambition found no fuel for her fire,
He had what God could give or man desire,
Till pity roused him from his soft repose,
His life to unseen hazards to expose;
Till pity moved him in our cause to appear,
Pity! that word which now we hate to hear;
But English gratitude is always such,
To hate the hand that does oblige too much.

BRITANNIA'S cries gave birth to his intent,
And hardly gain'd his unforeseen assent;
His boding thoughts foretold him he should find
The people fickle, selfish, and unkind;
Which thought did to his royal heart appear
More dreadful than the dangers of the war;
For nothing grates a generous mind so soon,
As base returns for hearty service done.

SATIRE, be silent! awfully prepare
Britannia's song, and William's praise to hear;
Stand by, and let her cheerfully rehearse
Her grateful vows in her immortal verse.
Loud fame's eternal trumpet let her sound,
Listen, ye distant poles, and endless round,
May the strong blast the welcome news convey,
As far as sound can reach or spirit fly!
To neighb'ring worlds, if such there be, relate
Our heroes fame for theirs to imitate;
To distant worlds of spirits let her rehearse,
For spirits without the helps of voice converse:
May angels hear the gladsome news on high,
Mix'd with their everlasting symphony;
And hell itself stand in surprise to know,
Whether it be the fatal blast or no.

BRITANNIA.

THE fame of virtue 'tis for which I sound,
And heroes with immortal triumphs crown'd;
Fame built on solid virtue swifter flies,
Than morning light can spread the eastern skies:
The gath'ring air returns the doubling sound;
And loud repeating thunders force it round;
Echoes return from caverns of the deep,
Old Chaos dreams on't in eternal sleep:
Time hands it forward to its latest urn,
From whence it never, never shall return:
Nothing is heard so far, or lasts so long,
'Tis heard by ev'ry ear, and spoke by every tongue.

MY hero, with the sails of honour furl'd,
Rises like the great genius of the world;

By fate and fame wisely prepared to be
The soul of war and life of victory;
He spreads the wings of virtue on the throne,
And ev'ry wind of glory fans them on;
Immortal trophies dwell upon his brow,
Fresh as the garlands he has won but now.

BY different steps the high ascent he gains,
And differently that high ascent maintains:
Princes for pride and lust of rule make war,
And struggle for the name of conqueror;
Some fight for fame, and some for victory,
He fights to save, and conquers to set free.

THEN seek no phrase his titles to conceal,
And hide with words what actions must reveal;
No parallel from Hebrew stories take,
Of godlike kings my similes to make;
No borrowed names conceal my living theme,
But names and things directly I proclaim;
His honest merit does his glory raise,
Whom that exalts let no man fear to praise;
Of such a subject no man need be shy,
Virtue's above the reach of flattery;
He needs no character but his own fame,
Nor any flattering titles but his own name.

WILLIAM'S the name that's spoke by every tongue,
William's the darling subject of my song;
Listen, ye virgins, to the charming sound,
And in eternal dances hand it round;
Your early offerings to this altar bring,
Make him at once a lover and a king;
May he submit to none but to your arms,
Nor ever be subdued, but by your charms;
May your soft thoughts for him be all sublime,
And ev'ry tender vow be made for him;
May he be first in ev'ry morning thought,
And heav'n ne'er hear a prayer where he's left out;
May every omen, every boding dream,
Be fortunate by mentioning his name;
May this one charm infernal powers affright,
And guard you from the terror of the night;

May ev'ry cheerful glass as it goes down
To William's health, be cordials to your own:
Let ev'ry song be chorust with his name,
And music pay her tribute to his fame;
Let ev'ry poet tune his artful verse,
And in immortal strains his deeds rehearse:
And may Apollo never more inspire
The disobedient bard with his seraphic fire
May all my sons their grateful homage pay,
His praises sing, and for his safety pray.

SATIRE, return to our unthankful isle,
Secured by heaven's regards, and William's toil:
To both ungrateful, and to both untrue,
Rebels to God, and to good nature too.

IF e'er this nation be distress'd again,
To whomsoe'er they cry, they'll cry in vain;
To heav'n they cannot have the face to look,
Or, if they should, it would but heav'n provoke;
To hope for help from man would be too much,
Mankind would always tell 'em of the Dutch:
How they came here our freedoms to maintain,
Were paid, and cursed, and hurried home again;
How by their aid we first dissolved our fears,
And then our helpers damn'd for foreigners:
'Tis not our English temper to do better,
For Englishmen think ev'ry one their debtor.

'TIS worth observing, that we ne'er complain'd
Of foreigners, nor of the wealth we gain'd,
Till all their services were at an end:
Wise men affirm it is the English way,
Never to grumble till they come to pay;
And then they always think, their temper's such,
The work too little, and the pay too much.

AS frighted patients, when they want a cure,
Bid any price, and any pain endure:
But when the doctor's remedies appear,
The cure's too easy, and the price too dear:
Great Portland near was banter'd when he strove,
For us his master's kindest thoughts to move:

We ne'er lampoon'd his conduct, when employ'd
King James's secret councils to divide:
Then we caress'd him as the only man,
Who could the doubtful oracle explain;
The only Hushai, able to repel
The dark designs of our Achitophel:
Compared his master's courage to his sense,
The ablest statesman, and the bravest prince;
On his wise conduct we depended much,
And liked him ne'er the worse for being Dutch:
Nor was he valued more than he deserved,
Freely he ventured, faithfully he served;
In all King William's dangers he has shared,
In England's quarrels always he appear'd:
The revolution first, and then the Boyne,
In both, his counsels and his conduct shine;
His martial valour Flanders will confess,
And France regrets his managing the peace;
Faithful to England's interest and her king,
The greatest reason of our murmuring:
Ten years in English service he appear'd,
And gain'd his master's and the world's regard;
But 'tis not England's custom to reward,
The wars are over, England needs him not;
Now he's a Dutchman, and the Lord knows what.

SCHONBERGH, the ablest soldier of his age,
With great Nassau did in our cause engage;
Both join'd for England's rescue and defence,
The greatest captain and the greatest prince;
With what applause his stories did we tell,
Stories which Europe's volumes largely swell!
We counted him an army in our aid,
Where he commanded, no man was afraid;
His actions with a constant conquest shine,
From Villa Vitiosa to the Rhine;
France, Flanders, Germany, his fame confess,
And all the world was fond of him but us:
Our turn first served, we grudged him the command,
Witness the grateful temper of the land.

WE blame the King, that he relies too much,
On Strangers, Germans, Hugonots, and Dutch;

And seldom does his great affairs of state,
To English counsellors communicate:
The fact might very well be answer'd thus:
He had so often been betray'd by us,
He must have been a madman to rely,
On English gentlemen's fidelity;
For, laying other argument aside:
This thought might mortify our English pride;
That foreigners have faithfully obey'd him,
And none but Englishmen have e'er betray'd him:
They have our ships and merchants bought and sold,
And barter'd English blood for foreign gold;
First to the French they sold our Turkey fleet,
And injured Talmarsh next at Cameret;
The king himself is shelter'd from their snares,
Not by his merits, but the crown he wears;
Experience tells us 'tis the English way,
Their benefactors always to betray.

AND, lest examples should be too remote,
A modern magistrate of famous note,
Shall give you his own history by rote;
I'll make it out, deny it he that can,
His worship is a true-born Englishman;
By all the latitude that empty word,
By modern acceptation's understood:
The parish books his great descent record,
And now he hopes ere long to be a lord;
And truly, as things go, it would be pity,
But such as he bore office in the city;
While robb'ry for burnt-offering he brings,
And gives to God what he has stole from kings;
Great monuments of charity he raises,
And good St. Magnus whistles out his praises;
To city jails he grants a jubilee,
And hires huzza's from his own mobile.

LATELY he wore the golden chain and gown,
With which equipp'd he thus harangued the town.

HIS FINE SPEECH, &c.

WITH clouted iron shoes, and sheep-skin breeches,
More rags than manners, and more dirt than riches,
From driving cows and calves to Leyton market,
While of my greatness there appear'd no spark yet,
Behold I come to let you see the pride,
With which exalted beggars always ride.

BORN to the needful labours of the plough,
The cart-whip graced me, as the chain does now.
Nature and fate in doubt what course to take,
Whether I should a lord or plough-boy make;
Kindly at last resolv'd they would promote me,
And first a knave, and then a knight they vote me.
What fate appointed, nature did prepare,
And furnish'd me with an exceeding care,
To fit me for what they design'd to have me;
And every gift but honesty they gave me.

AND thus equipp'd, to this proud town I came,
In quest of bread, and not in quest of fame.
Blind to my future fate, an humble boy,
Free from the guilt and glory I enjoy.
The hopes which my ambition entertain'd,
Where in the name of foot-boy, all contain'd.
The greatest heights from small beginnings rise;
The gods were great on earth, before they reach'd the skies.

BACKWELL, the generous temper of whose mind,
Was always to be bountiful inclin'd:
Whether by his ill fate or fancy led,
First took me up, and furnish'd me with bread:
The little services he put me to,
Seem'd labours, rather than were truly so.
But always my advancement he design'd;
For 'twas his very nature to be kind:
Large was his soul, his temper ever free;
The best of masters and of men to me:
And I who was before decreed by fate,
To be made infamous as well as great,
With an obsequious diligence obey'd him,
Till trusted with his all, and then betray'd him.

ALL his past kindnesses I trampled on,
Ruin'd his fortunes to erect my own:
So vipers in the bosom bred begin,
To hiss at that hand first which took them in;
With eager treach'ry I his fall pursu'd,
And my first trophies were ingratitude.

INGRATITUDE'S the worst of human guilt,
The basest action mankind can commit;
Which, like the sin against the Holy Ghost,
Has least of honour, and of guilt the most;
Distinguished from all other crimes by this,
That 'tis a crime which no man will confess;
That sin alone, which should not be forgiv'n
On earth, altho' perhaps it may in heaven.

THUS my first benefactor I o'erthrew;
And how shou'd I be to a second true?
The public trust came next into my care,
And I to use them scurvily prepare:
My needy sov'reign lord I play'd upon,
And lent him many a thousand of his own;
For which great interest I took care to charge,
And so my ill-got wealth became so large.

MY predecessor Judas was a fool,
Fitter to have been whipt and sent to school,
Than sell a Saviour: had I been at hand,
His Master had not been so cheap trepann'd;
I would have made the eager Jews have found,
For thirty pieces, thirty thousand pound.

MY cousin Ziba, of immortal fame,
(Ziba and I shall never want a name:)
First-born of treason, nobly did advance
His Master's fall, for his inheritance:
By whose keen arts old David first began
To break his sacred oath to Jonathan:
The good old king 'tis thought was very loth
To break his word, and therefore broke his oath.
Ziba's a traitor of some quality,
Yet Ziba might have been inform'd by me:

Had I been there, he ne'er had been content
With half th' estate, nor half the government.

IN our late revolution 'twas thought strange,
That I of all mankind should like the change,
But they who wonder'd at it never knew,
That in it I did my old game pursue:
Nor had they heard of twenty thousand pound,
Which ne'er was lost, yet never could be found.

THUS all things in their turn to sale I bring,
God and my master first, and then the king;
Till by successful villanies made bold,
I thought to turn the nation into gold;
And so to forgery my hand I bent,
Not doubting I could gull the Government;
But there was ruffl'd by the Parliament.
And if I 'scaped th' unhappy tree to climb,
'Twas want of law, and not for want of crime;

BUT my old friend,[A] who printed in my face
A needful competence of English brass;
Having more business yet for me to do,
And loth to lose his trusty servant so,
Managed the matter with such art and skill,
As sav'd his hero, and threw out the Bill.

AND now I'm grac'd with unexpected honours,
For which I'll certainly abuse the donors:
Knighted, and made a tribune of the people,
Whose laws and properties I'm like to keep well:
The custos rotulorum of the city,
And captain of the guards of their banditti.
Surrounded by my catchpoles, I declare
Against the needy debtor open war.
I hang poor thieves for stealing of your pelf,
And suffer none to rob you, but myself.

THE king commanded me to help reform ye,
And how I'll do't, Miss —— shall inform ye.
I keep the best seraglio in the nation,
And hope in time to bring it into fashion;

- 36 -

No brimstone whore need fear the lash from me,
That part I'll leave to Brother Jefferey:
Our gallants need not go abroad to Rome,
I'll keep a whoring jubilee at home;
Whoring's the darling of my inclination;
An't I a magistrate for reformation?
For this my praise is sung by ev'ry bard,
For which Bridewell wou'd be a just reward.
In print my panegyric fills the street,
And hired gaol-birds their huzzas repeat;
Some charities contriv'd to make a show,
Have taught the needy rabble to do so;
Whose empty noise is a mechanic fame,
Since for Sir Beelzebub they'd do the same.

THE CONCLUSION.

THEN let us boast of ancestors no more,
Or deeds of heroes done in days of yore,
In latent records of the ages past,
Behind the rear of time, in long oblivion plac'd;
For if our virtues must in lines descend,
The merit with the families would end,
And intermixtures would most fatal grow;
For vice would be hereditary too;
The tainted blood would of necessity,
Involuntary wickedness convey.

VICE, like ill-nature, for an age or two,
May seem a generation to pursue;
But virtue seldom does regard the breed,
Fools do the wise, and wise men fools succeed.

WHAT is't to us, what ancestors we had?
If good, what better? or what worse, if bad?
Examples are for imitation set,
Yet all men follow virtue with regret.

COULD but our ancestors retrieve their fate,
And see their offspring thus degenerate;
How we contend for birth and names unknown,

And build on their past actions, not our own;
They'd cancel records, and their tombs deface,
And openly disown the vile degenerate race:
For fame of families is all a cheat,
It's personal virtue only makes us great.

FOOTNOTES

[A] The Devil.

THE END.

Milton Keynes UK
Ingram Content Group UK Ltd.
UKHW040840141024
449705UK00006B/389